OCTOPUS ACROBATICS

Sue Fliess

illustrated by
Gareth Lucas

Albert Whitman & Company
Chicago, Illinois

Underneath the ocean's waves,
deep in coral reefs or caves,

Octopuses are invertebrates, or animals without backbones, that live in every ocean and along every US coast. There are about 300 species.

wedged in crevices or shells,
a fascinating creature dwells.

They spend much of their time in dens—hidden homes that could be small holes and crevices in rocks and coral. Some octopuses make holes in the sand or mud to hide.

Octopuses are usually alone and fiercely protect their homes.

Eight strong arms, no bones...how odd!
Alien? No, cephalopod!

A cephalopod is a sea animal that's a kind of mollusk, without a shell. It propels itself through the water, has muscular arms (often with suckers), eyes, and, usually, an ink sac that it squirts for defense.

An octopus can twist, stretch, curl its arms, and reach into holes to snatch prey. Its soft body is divided into parts. Because it doesn't have a shell, it can usually fit through any space larger than its beak.

Intelligent and so surprising,
the octopus is mesmerizing!

The wolfi octopus is the smallest octopus, less than one inch long and weighing less than a quarter of an ounce.

Some are giant, some petite,
some can grow to thirty feet!

The giant Pacific octopus is the largest, growing up to 20 feet in just three years. It's one of Earth's fastest-growing animals.

In its head are three small hearts
to pump blue blood around its parts.

Two hearts pump blood to gills. The gills take oxygen the octopus needs to breathe from the water. The third, larger heart pumps blood to the rest of the body.

Many suckers help it feel.
A beak to crunch on every meal.

An octopus grabs prey using its arms and strong suckers, then pulls the prey towards its beak.

Octopuses have great vision and can tell the size, shape, and brightness of objects, but they cannot see color.

Octopuses use their suckers to both taste and grip their food. The largest suckers can lift up to 30 pounds! A Pacific octopus has about 2,000 suckers.

Nine small brains to think things through...
just what *can't* this mollusk do?

In addition to the brain in its head, an octopus has a small brain in each of its eight arms. These small brains are groups of nerve cells that biologists say control movement.

Sleeping soundly through the day,
night's the time to hunt and play.

Camouflaging in plain sight,
waiting till the moment's right.

Planning for a sneak attack,
an octopus then grabs a snack.

When fish, shrimp, lobsters, or other food swims by, an octopus reaches out with an arm to stop and grip its prey with its suckers. Then it injects the prey with venom, or poison.

If the octopus needs more,
it may hunt along the shore.

Some octopuses occasionally leave the water to search for food and can survive on land for 20 to 30 minutes.

But sometimes it's the other way:
the octopus becomes the prey.

Changing color, texture, size,
it's a master of disguise.

Octopuses camouflage themselves to sneak up on prey or hide from predators. They can change shape, color, texture, pattern, and size.

Flashing, pulsing, swelling, shrinking,
swirling, swaying, shifting, blinking!

They also use color to show their mood: pale when stressed and bright red when mad.

They can create all kinds of patterns, including spots and stripes. Their skin can change color within milliseconds to match their environment.

Will it fight or flee or trick?
It must make decisions quick.

Sensing an approaching threat,
it stays as still as it can get.

Both the mimic and wonderpus octopus imitate dangerous animals including stingrays, lionfish, and sea snakes. This allows them to swim through or past their enemies undetected. They can even make themselves look like seaweed.

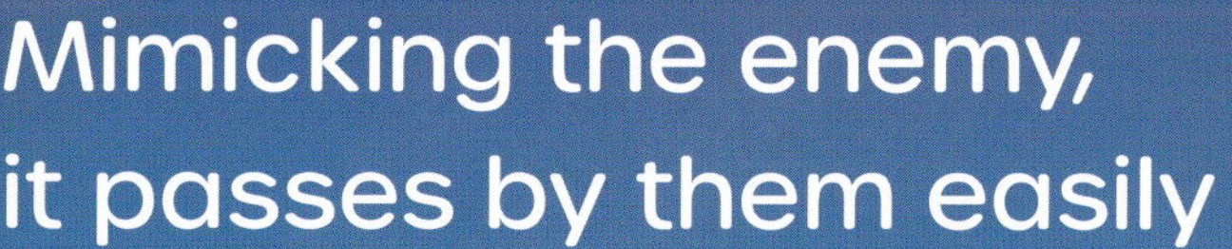

Mimicking the enemy,
it passes by them easily

or squirts its ink then jets away
and lives to see another day.

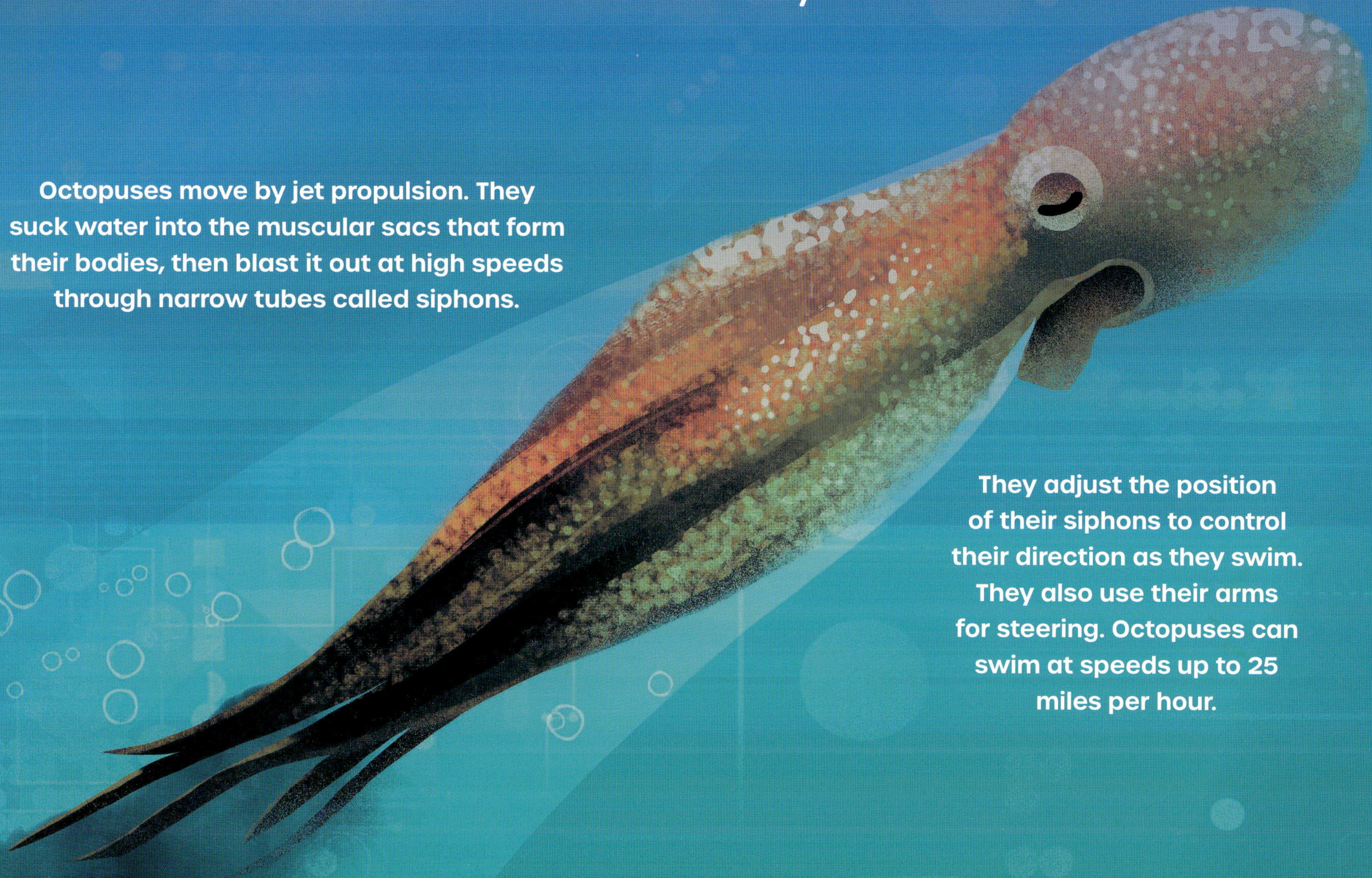

Octopuses move by jet propulsion. They suck water into the muscular sacs that form their bodies, then blast it out at high speeds through narrow tubes called siphons.

They adjust the position of their siphons to control their direction as they swim. They also use their arms for steering. Octopuses can swim at speeds up to 25 miles per hour.

When threatened, octopuses squirt big, dark clouds of poisonous ink into the water. The ink is usually black, brown, or dark red. It irritates predators' eyes and numbs their sense of smell.

On the move and unconfined,
an octopus is hard to find.

Skilled at playing hide-and-seek
in holes no bigger than its beak.

Octopuses don't stay in one place for very long. They may need to find a new food source, or they may be escaping nearby predators.

A 600-pound octopus can squeeze through an opening the size of a quarter.

Uses shells like tools to hide,
or hops a jellyfish to ride.

Veined octopuses sometimes carry and shelter inside of coconut shells when predators come near.

Octopuses can ride jellyfish. The blanket octopus sometimes tears a stinging tentacle off a Portuguese man-of-war to use as a weapon to defend itself.

It remembers things...it's true—
places, faces, old and new.

Inquisitive, it seeks connection—
hugs and holds to show affection.

Invertebrates such as octopuses can feel emotions such as curiosity, affection, and excitement. Divers have said they've befriended octopuses in the water, and when they've returned to the same dive spots, the octopuses recognize and remember them.

Impossible though it might seem, an octopus may even dream.

When octopuses have "quiet" sleep, they're pale and still. During "active" sleep, they can change color, pattern, or texture.

Females lay between 50 and 100,000 eggs in shelters under rocks or in holes. Or they hide their eggs in dens, stitching the eggs into hanging braids and then using a glue-like material to stick them to rocks so they don't wash away.

From birth until they're fully grown,
octopuses live alone,

only mating once, and then
they go their separate ways again.

Females stay with their eggs for two to fourteen months, until they hatch, moving water currents across the eggs to clean them and give them oxygen. Octopuses have short lives of one to four years.

She builds a den, lays eggs inside,
safe from predator and tide.

Soon they're hatching, one by one.
She starts to die. Her work is done.

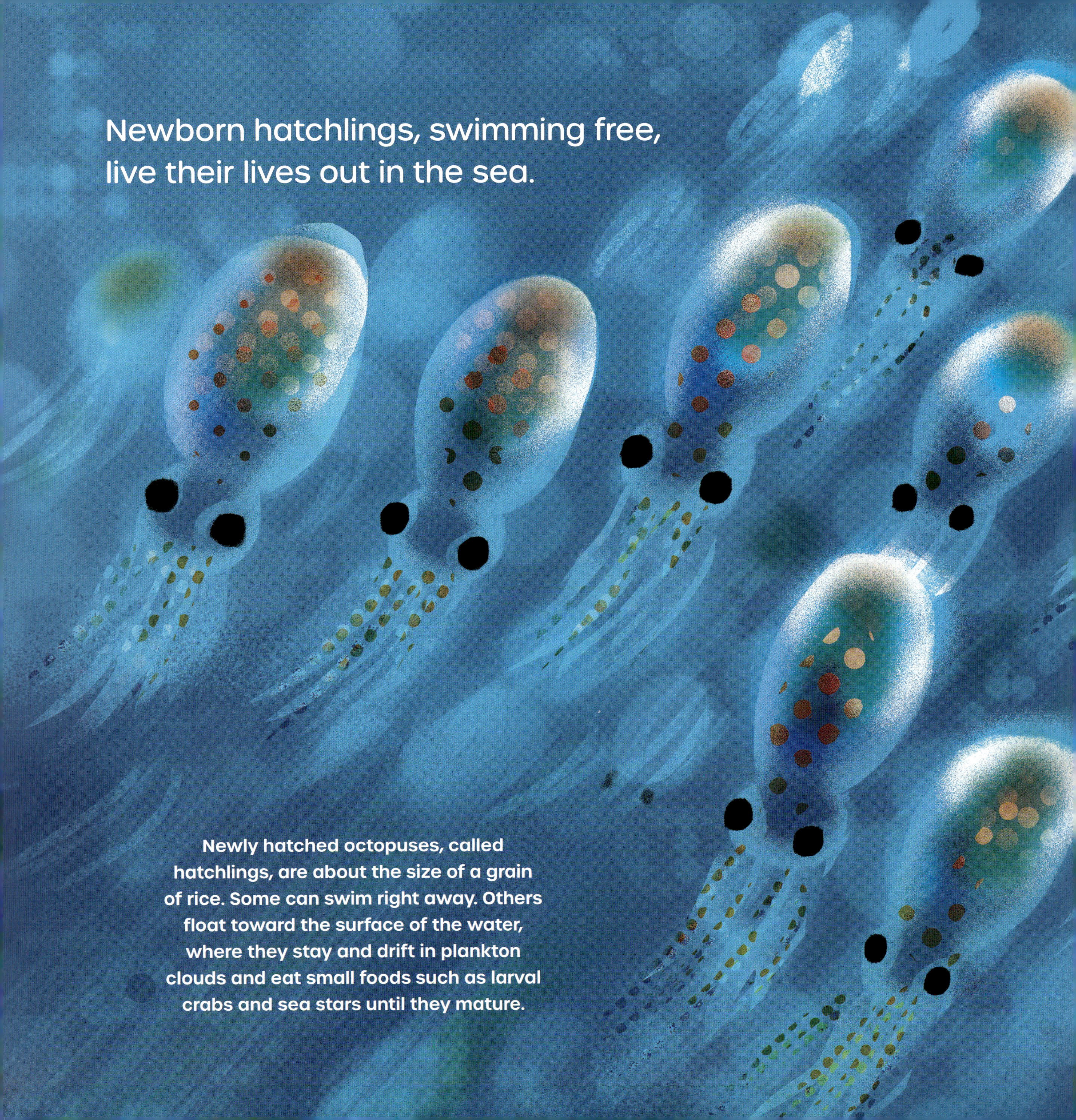

Newborn hatchlings, swimming free,
live their lives out in the sea.

Newly hatched octopuses, called hatchlings, are about the size of a grain of rice. Some can swim right away. Others float toward the surface of the water, where they stay and drift in plankton clouds and eat small foods such as larval crabs and sea stars until they mature.

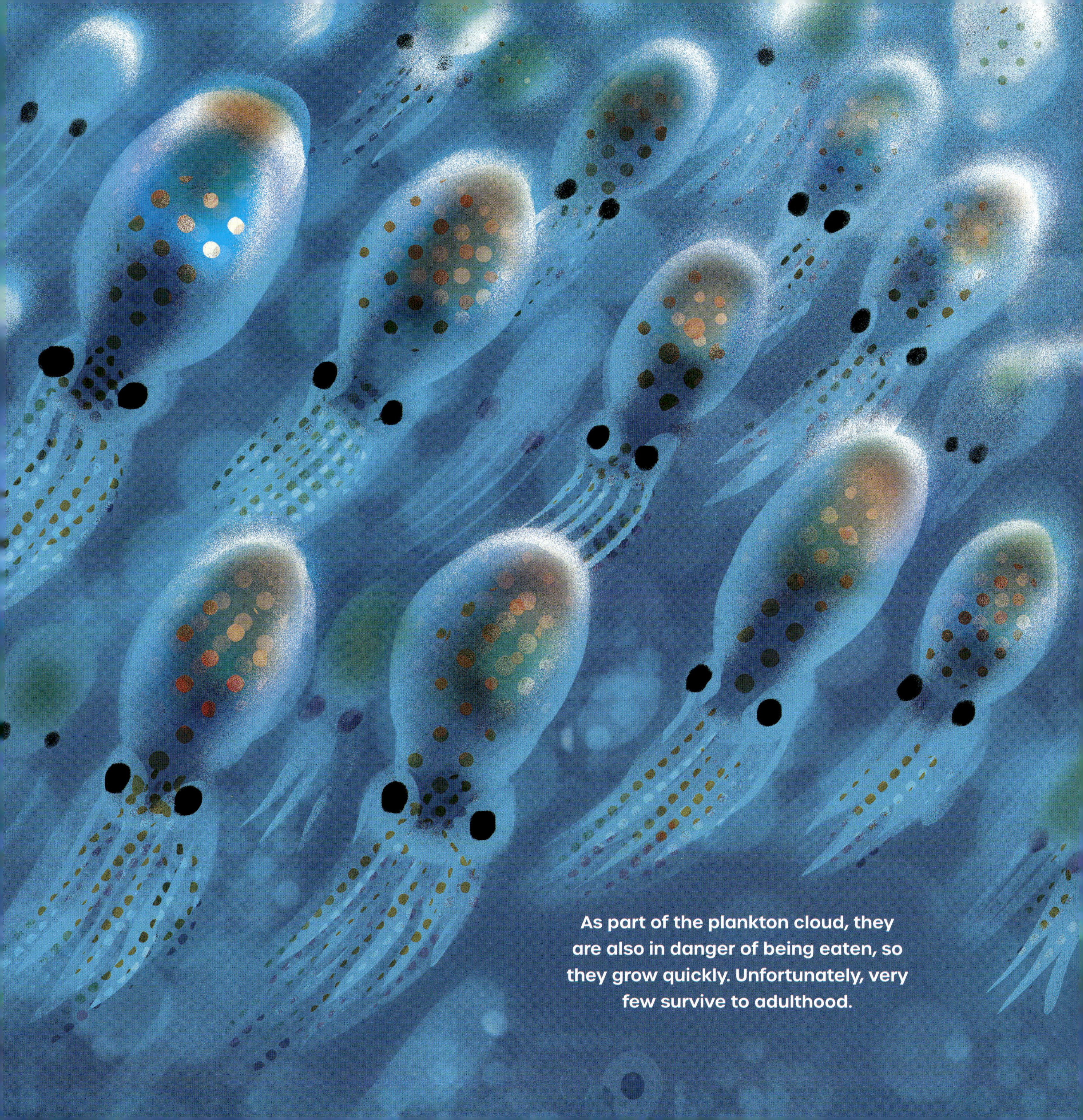

As part of the plankton cloud, they are also in danger of being eaten, so they grow quickly. Unfortunately, very few survive to adulthood.

Once a creature greatly feared,
now respected and revered.

Clever, strange, and marvelous, behold, the wondrous octopus!

Many years ago, when fishermen spotted large octopuses or squids from their boats, they would spear them out of fear, thinking they were sea monsters. Over time, scientists began to understand octopuses are highly intelligent creatures that are not a threat to people.

Glossary

camouflage: A defense or tactic that living things use to disguise their appearance, usually to blend in with their surroundings. It allows prey to avoid predators and predators to sneak up on prey.

hatchling: A newborn or newly hatched octopus.

mantle: The large, bag-shaped, muscular structure behind an octopus's head that holds body parts that carry out functions such as digesting food.

mollusk: An animal with a soft body but no backbone that usually has a shell and lives in water or damp places.

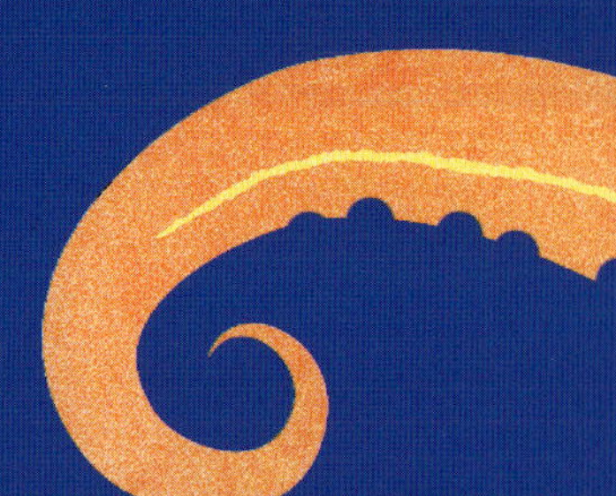

Author's Note

I have been curious about the ocean's creatures for as long as I can remember. I snorkeled for the first time as a very young girl, and seeing tropical fish swimming all around me was amazing. I've seen octopuses a few times at aquariums and two times in the wild; once, our guide rested an octopus's tentacle on my arm. The suckers are strong! Every encounter with these creatures was fascinating, and I'm blown away by their intelligence and uniqueness. Researching and writing this book was an absolute joy.

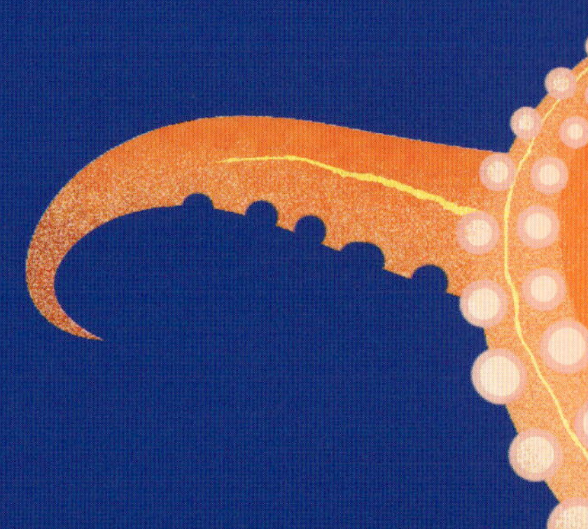

Children's Reference Books

Drimmer, Stephanie Warren. *Ink!*, Washington, DC: National Geographic Kids, 2019.

Montgomery, Sy. *The Octopus Scientists: Exploring the Mind of a Mollusk*. Boston: Houghton Mifflin Harcourt, 2015.

head
two large eyes
mantle
brain
three hearts
gill
beak
siphon
eight arms with two rows
of suction cups, or suckers

For Elfi and Maurice, may we never lose our sense of awe—SF

O LORD, how manifold are your works!
In wisdom have you made them all;
the earth is full of your creatures. Ps 104:24—GL

Library of Congress Cataloging-in-Publication data is on file with the publisher.

Illustrations by Gareth Lucas
Hardcover edition first published in the United States of America in 2024 by Albert Whitman & Company
Paperback edition first published in the United States of America in 2026 by Albert Whitman & Company

ISBN 978-0-8075-5816-4 (paperback)
ISBN 978-0-8075-5819-5 (ebook)

Printed in China
10 9 8 7 6 5 4 3 2 1 CM 30 29 28 27 26

Design by Rick DeMonico

For more information about Albert Whitman & Company,
visit our website at www.albertwhitman.com